BUILDING THE
Golden Gate
BRIDGE

An Interactive Engineering Adventure

by Blake Hoena

Consultant:
Karen C. Chou, PhD., P.E., F.ASCE
Clinical Professor, Department of Civil & Environmental Engineering
Northwestern University

CAPSTONE PRESS
a capstone imprint

You Choose Books are published by Capstone Press,
1710 Roe Crest Drive, North Mankato, Minnesota 56003
www.capstonepub.com

Library of Congress Cataloging-in-Publication Data
Hoena, B. A., author.
  Building the Golden Gate Bridge : an interactive engineering adventure / by Blake Hoena.
    pages cm.—(You choose. Engineering marvels)
  Summary:"Explores various perspectives on the process of building the Golden Gate Bridge. The
reader's choices reveal the historical details"—Provided by publisher.
  Audience: Ages 8–12.
  Audience: Grades 4 to 6.
  ISBN 978-1-4914-0398-3 (library binding)
  ISBN 978-1-4914-0403-4 (paperback)
  ISBN 978-1-4914-0407-2 (ebook PDF)
1. Golden Gate Bridge (San Francisco, Calif.)—Design and construction—Juvenile literature. 2.
Golden Gate Bridge (San Francisco, Calif.)—History—Juvenile literature. 3. Bridges—Design and
construction—Juvenile literature. I. Title.
  TG25.S225H64 2015
  624.2'30979461—dc23   2013047699

Editorial Credits
Adrian Vigliano, editor; Veronica Scott, designer; Wanda Winch, media researcher; Laura Manthe,
production specialist

Photo Credits
AP Images, 77; Bruce Cooper Collection, 9; Corbis: Roger Ressmeyer, 104, San Francisco
Chronicle, 100; Courtesy of the Bancroft Library/University of California, Berkeley, 37, 62, 68, 72,
79; Courtesy Scotts Bluff National Monument: William Henry Jackson, 6; Courtesy, California
Historical Society, CHS2011.734, 20; Getty Images/Imagno, 46, Underwood Archives, cover
(bottom left), 98; Library of Congress: Prints and Photographs Division, cover (middle), 29, 45;
National Parks Service/Fort Point-Golden Gate, 16; San Francisco History Center, San Francisco
Public Library, 12, 32, 55, 57, 83, 92, 102, International News Photo, 96, Moulin Studios, 86;
Shutterstock: alekup, Andre Nantel, 24, graph paper design element, grunge parchment sheet with
blueprint design, Scociologas

Printed in Canada.
032014   008086FRF14

TABLE OF CONTENTS

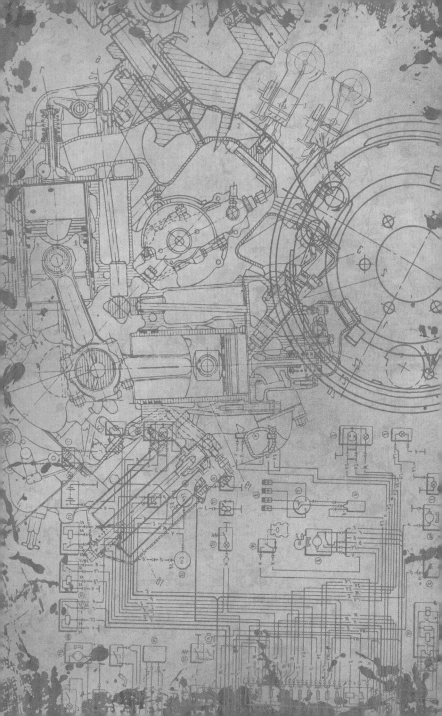

ABOUT YOUR ADVENTURE

YOU live in the exciting days of the early 1900s. Amazing new bridges and structures are being constructed. The boldest project yet is starting up— a bridge across California's Golden Gate strait. What part will you play in this great undertaking?

In this book you'll explore how the choices people made meant the difference between life and death. The events you'll experience happened to real people.

Chapter One sets the scene. Then you choose which path to read. Follow the directions at the bottom of each page. The choices you make will change your outcome. After you finish one path, go back and read the others for new perspectives and more adventures.

*YOU CHOOSE the path
you take through history.*

While building a sawmill for Captain John Sutter at Sutter's Mill, James Marshall spotted several gold flakes in the river water. He tried to keep his discovery secret, but word spread. These few flakes had triggered the California Gold Rush of 1849.

SPANNING THE GOLDEN GATE

When James Marshall discovered gold at Sutter's Mill in 1848, people from around the world flocked to California. After the discovery of silver in 1859 in neighboring Nevada, the region was booming. Many hopeful fortune seekers chose to brave the dangers of venturing west by land. For the tens of thousands who chose to travel by boat, the small village of San Francisco was often their destination.

Turn the page.

The rising population spurred economic growth, creating a demand for new businesses. Hotels and restaurants opened to house and feed newcomers. Then came banks and factories. In 1860 the population of the San Francisco Bay area was slightly more than 100,000. Fifty years later, it had risen to about 1 million.

During this time period, Henry Ford popularized the Model T car. It was the first affordable car for an average family. By 1910 more than 40,000 cars were sputtering along California's roads. In less than 10 years, that number grew to half a million.

All those cars began causing traffic problems. Roads needed to be paved. Bridges needed to be built. To San Francisco, with its growing population and booming economy, these were major issues.

San Francisco is surrounded by water on three sides, with the Pacific Ocean to the west and San Francisco Bay to the east. Connecting these two bodies of water is the Golden Gate, a three-mile strait forming the city's northern border.

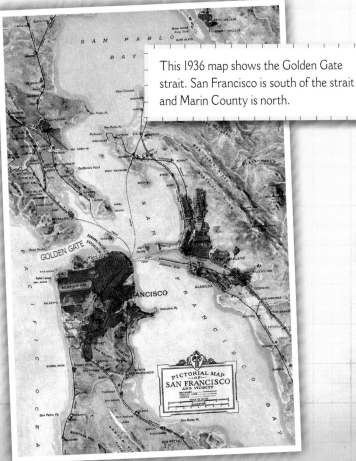

This 1936 map shows the Golden Gate strait. San Francisco is south of the strait and Marin County is north.

Turn the page.

Despite having jobs in San Francisco, many workers lived outside of the city where housing was more affordable. But with water all around, there were few ways for them to get in and out of the city. People in Marin County and other northern counties relied on ferries to carry them and their cars across the water. During the 1920s thousands traveled by ferry each day. Ferry services could barely keep up with demand. Sometimes it could take hours to get across the Bay. During busy holidays the trip could take days as cars backed up for miles and miles while waiting to board a ferry. Something had to be done.

In 1872 railroad executive Charles Crocker proposed a bridge spanning the Golden Gate. At the time such a bridge was thought to be impossible. The channel's narrowest spot, between Lime Point in Marin County and Fort Point in San Francisco, was more than 1 mile wide. But by the turn of the century, several large bridges had been constructed. None were as long as the Golden Gate Bridge would need to be, but they restored hope that a Golden Gate Bridge was possible.

You can play a role in this bold new project. The work will be a challenging test to your skills. It may be physically exhausting and even a threat to your life. But you could help to build something great if you're willing to take the risk.

To be an engineer in charge of your own bridge building company, turn to page 13.

To be a laborer seeking work on the Golden Gate Bridge project, turn to page 47.

Before the Golden Gate Bridge was built, Bay area residents relied on ferries to travel across the strait.

CHAPTER 2

DESIGNING THE BRIDGE

You are an engineer in charge of your own bridge building company. Since founding the Bascule Bridge Company in 1904, you have designed hundreds of bridges, mostly for railroads. Your ideas greatly improved the design of bascule bridges. These drawbridges have movable sections that lift to allow ships to pass underneath.

On August 26, 1916, one of your staff members tosses a copy of the San Francisco Call Bulletin on your desk.

"Read the Wilkins piece," she says.

Turn the page.

You turn to an article written by James Wilkins, a structural engineer turned newspaper editor. It starts, *"It is possible to bridge San Francisco Bay . . ."* You are both amazed and excited by what Wilkins wrote.

Because of your reputation, Michael O'Shaughnessy, San Francisco's city engineer, has been contracting you to build small bridges since 1915. You even have an office set up in San Francisco. During a 1919 trip there, O'Shaughnessy asks you to visit him. You know he has been talking to other designers about building a bridge over the Gate. You hope that this is what he wants to talk to you about. More than money, a project like that would bring you fame.

The morning before you meet with him, you head to the Golden Gate. You want to look at the site. You hike up a hill overlooking Fort Point. Gazing out across the strait, you are amazed by the scenery. Waves crash against the red, rocky shore below. Gusts of wind whip around, tossing your hair about. As the fog lifts, the sun spreads golden over the blue-green water. You see Lime Point on the opposite shore.

It would be difficult to build a bridge here, you admit to yourself, but you are confident in your abilities. *Give me enough money, and I can build a bridge to anywhere.*

Turn the page.

When you meet O'Shaughnessy, he starts by talking about the projects you are already working on. As he wraps up his questions, he walks over to his office window. He motions out toward the Bay.

"Everybody says it can't be done and that it would cost 100 million dollars if it could be done," he says.

This is an aerial view of the foggy Golden Gate strait in 1915. Marin County is visible at the top left of the photo.

You know he's referring to a Golden Gate bridge.

"No project is impossible," you say. "Look at the Brooklyn Bridge and the Williamsburg Bridge. They weren't thought possible at one time either."

"Yes, but the spans between their support towers are around 1,600 feet. This bridge would have to be twice that," O'Shaughnessy says.

"I'd guess just more than 4,000 feet," you say.

He smiles, as if he knows you've thought seriously about this project.

"What of the cost?" he asks.

To tell O'Shaughnessy that $100 million sounds about right, turn to page 18.

To tell O'Shaughnessy that you could build the bridge for much less, turn to page 22.

You tell him that you agree with his estimate. "I could provide you with a design," you say.

He seems hesitant. But he politely listens as you tell him about the challenges, from the depth of the water to the tons of steel needed.

"OK, show me what this bridge might look like," he says.

You rush back to your office in Chicago, excited to be working on such a grand project.

You begin to review some of the largest bridges built to date. The Brooklyn Bridge, built in 1883, was the first steel suspension bridge. Its middle span hangs from cables that are held by two support towers. It is flexible in the middle. That kind of flexibility would be important with the Bay's ever-changing winds and the earthquakes common in California.

Then there is Canada's Pont de Québec Bridge, built in 1919. It is a cantilever bridge. A cantilever bridge has a middle span held up by arms that are weighted and balanced on two supporting towers. With a span of 1,800 feet, it's the largest bridge built to date. It is also a strong and rigid style of bridge, which you feel is important because of the distance the Golden Gate Bridge would have to span.

You take ideas from both of these bridges and start drawing the Golden Gate Bridge. Eventually you travel back to San Francisco to present your design to O'Shaughnessy.

Turn the page.

"Well, what do you think?" you ask.
"Will this work?"

He nods hesitantly as he looks at the
cantilever-suspension bridge you designed.

This is Joseph Strauss' original
design for the Golden Gate Bridge
as a cantilever-suspension hybrid.

"I'm impressed by your unique design," he says. "But the cost is just too much. The Board of Supervisors for the city and county of San Francisco is only willing to commit $25 million to the project."

He seems ready to usher you out the door, but you aren't ready to give up.

"I have several other ideas that I could explore," you say. "Will you allow me to work on another design?"

He considers your request for a moment, then nods yes. You thank him and say good-bye. As you leave his office you're already trying to decide what to do.

To have experts review the cost of your cantilever-suspension design, turn to page 27.

To try a more traditional cantilever bridge design, turn to page 39.

"That's wonderful!" O'Shaughnessy says, thrilled at the idea of a less expensive design.

You head back to Chicago, excited about the project. But you realize that it presents some unique difficulties. The water in the strait is several hundred feet deep, and strong currents flow in and out on the tide. So you can't place the support towers too far from shore. The span between the towers will be twice as wide as any other bridge. Steel recently replaced cast iron as a stronger, lighter, and more durable building material. But a bridge this size would greatly test its capabilities.

One design option is a suspension bridge, which hangs from cables held by two support towers. The Williamsburg Bridge, built in 1903, is a good example, though its middle span is only 1,601 feet. But suspension bridges are economical, using fewer construction materials than other types of bridges. They are also flexible, which could be important with the Bay's ever-changing weather conditions and the earthquakes common in California.

The other option is a cantilever bridge, which has a middle span held up by arms that are weighted and balanced on two supporting towers.

Turn the page.

Canada's Pont de Québec Bridge, built in 1919, is the largest cantilever bridge. Its 1,800-foot span is the longest of any bridge in the world. Cantilevers are strong and rigid, traits you feel could also be important because of the distance the Golden Gate Bridge would have to span.

As you begin to develop a concept for the bridge, you realize both types of bridges have their pros and cons.

Canada's Pont de Québec bridge has been the world's longest cantilever bridge since 1919.

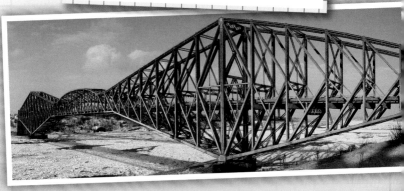

To present a suspension bridge design, go to page 25.

To present a hybrid bridge design, turn to page 27.

To present a cantilever bridge design, turn to page 39.

A little more than a year later, you present your design for a suspension bridge to O'Shaughnessy. Like the Williamsburg Bridge, it has two support towers that will be built just offshore. Those towers are connected by steel cables, which would hold up the roadway.

"A suspension bridge?" O'Shaughnessy says. He sounds unimpressed.

"I took the idea from the Wilkins article," you reply.

"Yes, yes, so have other bridge designers I've talked to," O'Shaughnessy says. "But while I was impressed with what Wilkins had to say, he is not an expert bridge designer. And you're not known for designing suspension bridges."

Turn the page.

His words are harsh, but what he says next gives you some hope.

"I'm not sure Mayor James Rolph or the Board of Supervisors for the city and county of San Francisco would approve of your design," he says. "After your ingenuity with bascule bridges, I was expecting something more unique from you."

"This is but one of several ideas I have," you say. "May I show you another one?"

"No one has presented an acceptable design yet," he says, "so yes."

26

You have two other ideas that you could show him.

To attempt a hybrid bridge design, go to page 27.

To revisit a cantilever bridge design, turn to page 39.

On June 28, 1921, after a review of the cost of your bridge, you present your cantilever-suspension design to O'Shaughnessy. It has two support towers with large cantilever arms made of steel girders balanced on top. But unlike a standard cantilever bridge, the arms don't reach all the way across the gap between the two towers. Rather, the arms are connected by two huge cables. From those cables hang smaller cables, which support the roadway.

"I've had several experts review this design," you say. "And they approve of it, estimating the cost to be about $17 million."

O'Shaughnessy nods and smiles happily.

Turn the page.

"Let me show this to Mayor James Rolph and the Board of Supervisors for the City and County of San Francisco," he says excitedly. "This design is unique and has potential."

You talk to O'Shaughnessy off and on over the next couple of years as you work on other projects in San Francisco. For the most part, he seems to feel confident in your design. But to help promote it further, you decide to hire Charles Alton Ellis, an engineering expert. He tirelessly works on tweaking your ideas. Mentioning Ellis' expertise also helps the Board of Supervisors trust your design.

Then in 1923 California organizes the Golden Gate Bridge and Highway District, a special area around the location where the bridge will be built. This allows San Francisco and Marin Counties to borrow money to build a bridge. But the War Department has concerns about whether a bridge will obstruct ship traffic, especially warships. During a hearing, you field questions from Colonel Herbert Deakyne of the Corps of Engineers.

New York's Williamsburg Bridge was the longest suspension bridge in the world from 1903 to 1924.

Turn the page.

"Is there a possibility that a ship could collide with one of the piers?" he asks.

"No," you reply. "The channel is wide enough for the piers to be about 4,000 feet apart."

"So there's no danger, not even in fog?" he asks.

"We will place lights on the bridge," O'Shaughnessy adds, coming to your defense. "They will actually aid in navigation."

With the War Department's approval, the project moves forward. You are officially hired on as its chief engineer in 1929, largely because of all the work that you've already done to help promote the project. While you have your staff from your company, the Board of Supervisors also hires a staff of experts to advise you. This Advisory Board of Engineers includes Leon Moisseiff, a leading expert in suspension bridge design; Othmar Hermann Ammann, designer of the George Washington Bridge; and Charles Derleth Jr., designer of the Carquinez Strait Highway Bridge.

Turn the page.

During your first meeting with them, Derleth confronts you.

"We have some concerns about your design," he says. "There are structural issues with the size of it. Perhaps we should consider a more traditional suspension bridge."

Joseph Strauss overcame many problems as chief engineer of the Golden Gate Bridge.

To change your design to a suspension bridge, go to page 33.

To proceed with your design, turn to page 41.

You heed the advice of your team.

In 1930 you propose a new design, a suspension bridge. New advances in making stronger, more durable steel helps you feel confident in this design. A suspension bridge would also be more flexible and adjust to the weather. According to Moisseiff and Ellis's calculations, it could move up and down by as much as 16 feet.

At first, O'Shaughnessy is surprised by the change, but after reviewing the new design, he seems relieved. There have been concerns about the cost of your original design. Some say it could exceed $112 million. Public opinion is also against anything that would mar the natural beauty of the Golden Gate, and your hybrid design was huge.

Turn the page.

Because of the new design, the bridge needs to be reapproved by the War Department. This allows those who oppose the bridge to speak out. Among them are shipping companies that worry a bridge will interfere with their business. At the hearing their attorney questions you.

"Will the tide cause the bridge to move?" he asks.

"Not the tide," you reply, "but the weather."

The room is quiet. Everyone is waiting for more information. You know the clearance for ships under the bridge will go up and down due to temperature, but mentioning this might cause more trouble with the shipping companies. Perhaps it would be better to shift the focus to the bridge's flexibility against gusts of wind.

To explain the changes caused by temperature, go to page 35.

To explain the changes caused by wind, turn to page 44.

"Because of the temperature," you say. "On hot days, the cables will lengthen and lower the bridge as much as 16 feet."

You look over to Major General Lytle Brown, who is presiding over this hearing, and your response seems to sway him. The War Department eventually approves the new design.

There are still a lot of people who oppose the bridge project. The owners of ferry companies worry that they will go out of business. People protest the taxes that will need to be raised to fund the project. But you argue that the ferry system cannot keep up with the growing traffic congestion. Ferries transport only about 1,000 vehicles an hour. Your six-lane bridge design could handle that number in a fraction of the time.

Turn the page.

In 1932 Amadeo P. Gianni, chairman of the board of Bank of America, pledges his bank's support. The project will be fully financed between money from the bank and new taxes.

On February 26, 1933, a parade is held to celebrate the beginning of construction. Tens of thousands of people come out to show their support for the bridge.

You lean over to William Filmer, president of the Golden Gate Bridge and Highway District, and say, "I wish people had been this enthusiastic for the bridge 10 years ago."

He chuckles as you both watch Mayor Angelo Rossi dig into the earth with a golden spade. He makes a short speech and then hands the shovel to Filmer, who does the same. Filmer hands you the shovel, and you quickly overturn a shovelful of dirt.

People around you celebrate. But you know that construction on the bridge really began a month earlier, when steam shovels started excavation for the foundation of the tower off Lime Point.

Each foundation had to be strong enough to support one of the bridge's massive 746-foot-tall towers.

Turn the page.

For the most part, your job is done. Now you can watch as the bridge's towers rise ever so slowly skyward. In four years there will be another celebration similar to this one. That will be for the bridge opening on May 27, 1937. Your name will be attached to one of the biggest construction projects of the 20th century.

THE END

To follow another path, turn to page 11.
To read the conclusion, turn to page 101.

As soon as you complete your cantilever design, you present it to O'Shaughnessy. It has two support towers with massive arms made of steel girders, balanced atop them.

O'Shaughnessy looks over your design and snorts.

"Are you serious?" he asks. "A cantilever bridge? It's monstrous."

"But it needs to be," you reply. "To span a gap nearly a mile long, we need a sturdy bridge, and cantilever bridges are the strongest built to date."

O'Shaughnessy shakes his head.

"Just imagine the cost of all that steel. The stain it will be on the scenery."

You feel defeated.

Turn the page.

As he ushers you out his office door, he adds, "I'm sorry, but Mayor James Rolph and the Board of Supervisors for the City and County of San Francisco would never approve this design."

That is the last time he speaks to you about the Golden Gate Bridge project. You continue to work on several smaller bridges throughout the city, but only watch, as years later, a bridge spanning the Gate slowly rises skyward. If only you had provided a better design, your name would be attached to the famous bridge.

THE END

To follow another path, turn to page 11.
To read the conclusion, turn to page 101.

You decide it's best to stick with your cantilever-suspension bridge design. After all, the Board of Supervisors approved of it. So did the War Department.

But then the public starts voicing their opinions. "It looks like an upside-down rat trap," you read in the newspapers. Many call it an eyesore and say that it will ruin the natural beauty of the Golden Gate.

On top of that, some experts suggest that the bridge could cost upwards of $112 million because of the huge amounts of steel needed. That is well above the newest budget of $35 million.

41

Turn the page.

Under the pressure of public opinion and finances, support for your design fades. You hear grumbling from the Board of Supervisors. O'Shaughnessy acts aloof whenever you try to discuss the project with him. Finally, you are called into a meeting with the mayor, the board, and O'Shaughnessy.

"I'm sorry," O'Shaughnessy starts, "But because of recent concerns regarding your bridge design, we need to ask you to step down as chief engineer."

This comes as quite a surprise to you, but the next words hurt even more.

"We're offering the position to Derleth, who has shown us a design for a suspension bridge."

If only you had followed your advisor's suggestion, you would have helped build the largest bridge in the world. Instead, you are headed back to your home office in Chicago, deflated.

THE END

To follow another path, turn to page 11.
To read the conclusion, turn to page 101.

"Because of the wind," you reply. "The bridge will need to be able to move because of gusts whipping through the Gate."

The attorney scoffs at this reply. "So the bridge will be like a swing?" he asks. "Wouldn't that be dangerous?"

"No, but ..." you start to reply as you glance over at Major General Lytle Brown, who is presiding over this hearing. You can tell he is unimpressed with your answer.

Approval for your design is eventually denied. And it's not until years later that you hear someone else was able to successfully pitch a bridge design that was approved.

THE END

To follow another path, turn to page 11.
To read the conclusion, turn to page 101.

By 1934 the north (Marin) tower was nearing completion.

By 1935 both towers were complete and the cable work had begun.

CHAPTER 3

CONSTRUCTING THE BRIDGE

In the beginning of the 1930s, people are feeling the pains of the Great Depression (1929–1939). In San Francisco alone nearly 1 in 4 people are out of work. You are among the unemployed. You can't afford toys or new clothes for your children. You can barely provide enough food to feed your family.

Jobs are scarce, but you know that one of the best opportunities for work is on the construction of the Golden Gate Bridge. The firms building it have agreed to hire mostly workers from around the Bay area.

Turn the page.

You have some construction experience, having worked on a few of the many smaller bridges built throughout San Francisco. So every morning, you wake early and walk from your home to the construction site of the Golden Gate Bridge. You are among hundreds of other job seekers who mill about outside the fenced-in area. You hope that someone won't show up for work, that someone will get fired, or that the building schedule falls behind so more workers are needed. The workers up in the towers must think you're like a school of piranhas, waiting for one of them to fall so a job opens up.

Then one day, a foreman looks in your direction.

"You," he says, pointing toward you.

Before anyone else can react or block your path, you dash to an entrance in the fence and push your way through.

"Afraid of heights?" he asks.

To say, "No, and I'm an experienced ironworker!" turn to page 50.

To say, "No, sir!" turn to page 71.

He looks impressed when you mention your experience as an ironworker.

"Ever work as a bridgeman?" he asks.

"Yes, sir," you reply. "On the Fourth Street a while back."

"Want to work on another bridge designed by Joseph Strauss?" he asks. "I need a catcher."

"Yes, sir," you say. "I've never missed a rivet thrown my way."

"Good," he says," because we had a catcher miss once. The rivet fell and punched a hole in a boat below. The bosses at Bethlehem Steel weren't happy about paying the bill to repair her."

You're thrilled to have a job, and you hear the pay is good—up to $11 per day for experienced ironworkers. You will start work tomorrow morning on the bridge's north tower. You learn that crews are working ahead to steam hammer the heavy steel beams into place. Your crew will come up from behind and seal the connections of the girders with rivets.

The next morning, you wake bright and early. You pack a paper-bag lunch. You'll be working hundreds of feet up on the north tower. It will take quite a while to get up to your work site, so there will be no coming down to eat.

Turn the page.

That day, to celebrate your new job, you pay to ride the bus down to the work site. When you get there, you are taken to an access road from Waldo Grade down to Lime Point. You are excited as you head out just offshore to the tower.

Months earlier, a concrete base had been completed for the tower. The steel beams were shipped in all the way from Pennsylvania, through the Panama Canal and to San Francisco. Barges carried the beams out to the tower, which was slowly rising up into the sky. You always expected the structure to be gray, but it's a dull red.

"That's the color of the protective paint to keep it from rusting," one of your crewmates tells you later.

Since construction on the tower has already begun, it is hundreds of feet tall when you join your crew. It looks like a huge, metal skeleton—nothing like the final drawings you've seen. But then, there's still a lot of work to be done.

As you meet up with your crew boss and the rest of your crew members, the boss nods to you.

"Look sharp today. I hear Russell Cone is on site," he says.

"Who's he?" you ask.

"The resident engineer overseeing construction," he replies.

Turn the page.

"Where's Strauss?" you ask. Secretly you had been hoping to meet Joseph Strauss, the famous designer behind the Golden Gate Bridge.

"Probably checking on the foundation for the south tower," he says. "Storms have been causing problems over that way."

Your crew takes an elevator up into the steel skeleton of the tower. Soon you realize that finding your work site isn't a simple task. When pieced together, the steel girders form cells similar to hundreds of small square metal boxes. You travel through them, climb up ladders, crawl through manholes, and cross 12-inch beams from one cell to another. You feel lost in a maze hundreds of feet in the air.

Once you find the cell you are working on, you are amazed by how quickly the job goes.

One crew member works the forge. With a pair of tongs, he picks up a rivet from a bucket. Then he holds it over the forge. Once it's glowing red hot at 1,900 degrees Fahrenheit, he flings it to you.

A "catcher" does exactly that, catches. With a large metal cup shaped like a funnel, you catch the rivet in midair.

Two workers on the north tower pass rivets using a bucket.

Turn the page.

You hold out your cup for another crew member to pick up the rivet with a pair of tongs. Quickly, before it cools, he slips the rivet into a hole that connects two metal beams. On the side with the round end of the rivet, one crew member steps up with a bucking bar. The bucking bar is a metal rod that has a small divot in one end where the head of the rivet fits. He holds the rivet in place while on the other side of the beam, a crew member pushes against the rivet with a hammer powered by compressed air.

Both men's arms shake as the hammer pounds the end of the rivet's staff down until it's rounded off. While all this is being done, the rivet cools and expands, forming a solid bond between the beams.

"Keep working!" the foreman shouts. "You've got at least 300 more to go before the work day is out." In all, about 600,000 rivets will be used to hold together each of the bridge's towers.

Rivet crews had to do hard work in awkward positions at dizzying heights.

Turn the page.

Workers above are hammering the steel beams into place. Every so often, one of the workers above drops a tool, a snack, a hard hat, or some other random thing. The wind up top whips around dangerously, and a strong gust could push someone off the tower. So things get dropped as workers reach for solid handholds, causing people below to suffer from scratches, bruises, and broken limbs.

One day as you're working, you hear a clang coming from above. You remember your crew boss telling you that looking down protects your head. But that noise seemed unusually loud. Maybe this time it would be best to look up so you can see what's coming and protect yourself.

To look up, go to page 59.
To look down, turn to page 61.

You look up to see what's falling. But between the glare of the sun and the maze of metal beams above you, you see nothing. Then an angry shape whistles in front of your face. It smacks you in the cheek, and stars explode in your head. You reel backward, and luckily, you were holding on to the beam next to you.

"You OK?" a crew member shouts.

You turn to him, and he looks fuzzy.

"I'm not sure," you say.

You feel wobbly in the knees.

Then your crew boss comes up to you.

"We need to get you to the nurse's station," he says.

Turn the page.

You are quickly guided down from the tower. You find out you have suffered a concussion, and the side of your face is badly bruised, but nothing is broken.

There haven't been any fatalities on the bridge yet, and you're thankful that your injuries weren't worse. Next time, you'll remember the rule to look down if something is falling from above. That way your hard hat can protect you.

You're laid up and unable to work for several weeks. Then you get permission to go back to work. But your injury has left you worried about the job's danger.

60

To go back to work, turn to page 62.

To quit work on the bridge because of the danger, turn to page 91.

You follow the advice of your crew boss and look down. You try to position your hard hat so it is between you and whatever is falling.

Suddenly, something clips the side of your helmet, but doesn't hit you.

"You OK?" one of your crewmates asks.

"Yeah," you say. "Did you see what it was?"

"Looked like a tin cup," he says.

"Just glad I didn't get any hot coffee spilled on me," you laugh, and then go back to work.

Turn the page.

After a while on the job your crewmate Frank doesn't show up for work. He's usually at the bucking bar, but you know he's been suffering from headaches and dizziness lately.

"Take over for Frank," your crew boss tells you.

Once the towers were complete, workers began to prepare for the cable spinning that would come next.

You've watched him do his job and have taken a couple tries at it. You feel confident that you can handle the bucking bar.

You watch one coworker at the forge heat up a rivet. He then tosses it to the catcher. As quickly as possible, the catcher shoves the rivet into the hole connecting the two beams in front of you. You place the bucking bar over the rounded end of the rivet and lean in with all your weight. You grit your teeth as the hammer is engaged, knocking you back a bit. Your bones are rattled and your muscles shake like jelly.

One down, 300 and some more to go, you think to yourself.

Then another rivet is ready.

Turn the page.

The job is tiring, but you switch now and then with your crew members to take a break from it. And while the job is exhausting, you find it rewarding. You watch in amazement as the rivets sizzle and release steam when they slide into the holes. As you lean in on the bucking bar, you can even smell the hot metals fusing.

Frank hasn't returned to work yet. You wonder if he lost his job. You hear about people being let go, especially when work is slow. Then they rejoin the masses of unemployed gathering outside the fences around the construction site.

64

After replacing Frank on the bucking bar for a while, you start to get some bad headaches. You think it's from the hammer's shaking and rattling.

To keep working, go to page 65.

To tell your crew boss that you're feeling sick, turn to page 68.

You decide to ignore the headaches and continue working. The Great Depression is causing many financial problems. You don't want to risk losing wages.

Over the next couple weeks, your symptoms worsen. You have trouble sleeping. You don't have much of an appetite. One day, as you're walking across a beam, you suddenly feel dizzy. You look down and the maze of girders spins below you.

"Look up! Look up!" a crew member shouts.

You do as he says, trying to focus on the metal girder in front of you until the spinning stops. Then, ever so slowly, you put one foot in front of the other, inching forward.

At the end of the beam, members of your crew reach out to steady you.

Turn the page.

Your foreman walks over to you and looks you up and down.

"Are you sick?" he asks. "You don't look fit to work."

"I'm not sure what's wrong," you reply.

He assigns someone to help you back down so that you can visit one of the staff nurses. There, you find out that you are suffering from lead poisoning. The protective paint on the metal beams is lead based. Every time a red-hot rivet hits that paint, it releases lead-filled steam, which you have been breathing in while leaning against the bucking bar.

Shortly after your incident, anyone who might be in danger of breathing in toxic fumes is required to wear a mask with a respirator. That, however, doesn't help you. Because you waited so long to report your symptoms, you have lasting health problems. It takes months for you to recover from the nerve and muscle damage you suffered. By the time you're feeling healthy again, work on the north tower is already finished.

Like many bridge workers, you can still go back to the construction site and hope to get another job. You consider your options, wondering if continuing to work on the Golden Gate Bridge is too risky of a choice.

To accept work on the roadway, turn to page 85.

To quit work on the bridge because of the danger, turn to page 91.

"Boss, I'm feeling off today," you tell your crew boss.

"Headaches, a little nausea?" he asks.

"Yeah, tired, too," you reply.

Hard hats and respirator masks helped keep riveters safe while working on the bridge.

"Head down to the nursing station," he tells you.

There, you find out that you have the early symptoms of lead poisoning.

"You aren't the only one," a nurse tells you. "That protective paint of the beams is lead based."

The steam released when the red-hot rivets hit the steel beams was filled with lead. You breathed in a little every time you leaned in with the bucking bar. No wonder you were getting sick. And no wonder Frank isn't back at work yet. He had been breathing in the fumes much longer than you. You are allowed some time off until your symptoms clear.

From then on anyone who might be exposed to fumes from the lead paint wears a mask with a respirator on it.

Turn the page.

In late spring of 1934, your work on the north tower is completed. You are glad to have been part of this historic work, but you also feel relieved to have escaped serious injury.

Some of your crewmates have taken jobs constructing the bridge's roadway. You need to find another job, but you're worried about the danger of continuing work on the Golden Gate.

To look for work on the roadway, turn to page 85.

To look for safer bridge projects, turn to page 91.

"Good," he says. "Because we need extra men to help spin the cables up top on the bridge. You're now working for Roebling Company."

You've had construction jobs before, but what you'll be doing is unlike anything you've ever done before. In fact, few bridge workers have ever done the job before. You'll be helping place the large cables that will connect the two towers. It's a job that will eventually earn the nickname "skywalker," because you'll be hundreds of feet in the air.

You are told that you'll receive some training and then start work as soon as that's done. You're excited to have a job, and you hear the pay is good.

Turn the page.

The morning of your first day of work, you wake and pack lunch. It takes quite a while to get up on the towers. There will be no coming down for lunch. You'll be eating hundreds of feet in the air.

Also, you need to decide what to wear to work on an early fall day in California.

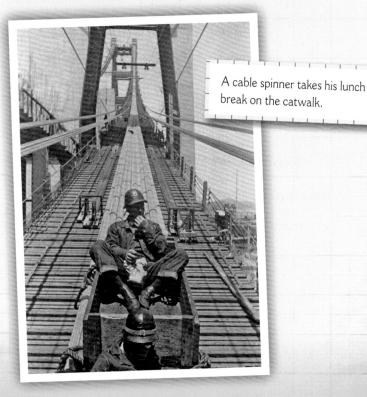

A cable spinner takes his lunch break on the catwalk.

To dress for cold weather, go to page 73.

To dress for warm weather, turn to page 89.

You grab your overalls, boots, and gloves. You also put on a sweater. While the mornings can be cool and foggy, things usually warm up during the day. But that's not necessarily true when you're hundreds of feet up in the air. Between the winds and cool seawater, you imagine things can get pretty chilly atop the bridge. You take a heavy coat as well.

At the construction site, you quickly find your crew boss. He looks you up and down.

"Good thing you brought that," he points to your coat. "It gets chilly up top."

He reaches under his sweater and pulls out a wad of newspaper.

"Here's a little trick I learned for keeping warm," he adds. "The morning newspaper."

He stuffs the newspaper back under his sweater. Then he hands you a plastic helmet.

"What's this for? Are we going to war already?" you joke.

"Nah, but everyone is supposed to wear one," he says.

"Really? I've never worn one on a construction job," you reply.

"You'd better put it on," your crew boss says. "I hear Russell G. Cone is on site."

"Who's he?" you ask.

"The resident engineer overseeing construction," he says.

"Ever see Strauss around here?" you ask. Secretly you had been hoping to meet Joseph Strauss, the famous designer behind the Golden Gate Bridge.

"Rumors are he hasn't been on site for months," he says.

You put on the helmet. You don't want to risk losing the job before you even start working. Then you go meet the rest of your crew. Soon you are riding an elevator up to the top of the bridge.

Turn the page.

Back in early August, the Golden Gate was closed for shipping as a single strand of wire rope was strung between the two towers. It was the first time that Lime Point and Fort Point had ever been connected. Beginning with that one wire, thousands of pencil-thin wires would follow.

Once up toward the top of the 756-foot tall tower, you are amazed by both the scenery and your working conditions. To the west, blue-green water stretches out endlessly, at least when you can see it through the fog. And from that very same direction come cold gusts of wind, which numb your fingers and redden your nose.

From the south tower that you are on to the north tower, catwalks have been strung out. They don't go straight from one tower to the next, but swoop down from where you are. Then at the center, each catwalk curves up to the top of the north tower. They follow the path that the wires are taking. There are rope railings on either side of the catwalks.

The completed catwalks stretched all the way from one tower to the other.

Turn the page.

When you join the crew, hundreds of wires have already been spun between the towers. But with the weather worsening as winter approaches, the crews are trying to speed up the pace. That's why you were hired.

Teams of men are stationed every 50 feet along the catwalk, and you are paired up with an experienced "skywalker." The job is somewhat complex. You watch as three wheels carrying a coil of wire each come racing down a guide rope. Sometimes you can see them coming. Other times, they just appear out of the fog before you, the cowbells attached to them jingling. Then you have to scramble to catch the wires.

A cable team works with a three-wheeled device used to carry wire strands across the strait.

Turn the page.

Once the wheels pass, you help gather, tighten, and keep the wires from twisting around one another. Once a large number of wires has been spun between the towers, they are bundled together. Overall, each of the huge cables strung between the two support towers will be made of 61 bundles of wires. Those bundles will contain many thousands of single wires.

"Why not just make one big bundle?" you ask one of the engineers overseeing the spinning of the cables.

"If there was just one cable connected to the middle of the anchor block, the weight would rip the fastening right out of the concrete," he explains. "So we're distributing the weight to 61 different spots on the block."

One day you're working up near the top of the north tower. It's a foggy morning, and you wait for the jingle of the cowbell to tell you that the wheels of wire are headed your way.

Sometimes as you work, the catwalk shifts and swings as gusts of wind hit it. As you're waiting, the catwalk bounces up and down, but so does the bundle of wires you've been working on.

"Never seen that happen before," your workmate says.

"Think we should check it out?" you ask.

"I don't know," he says. "Those wheels could come barreling down any second."

To go to the top of the tower to check on the bouncing wire bundles, turn to page 82.

To wait for the wheels, turn to page 92.

Working hundreds of feet up can be treacherous, and it feels like something is wrong.

"We'd better check it out," you tell your workmate.

"Fine, fine," he replies.

You trudge through the fog to the top of the tower. As you near the top, you hear muffled cries for help through the whistling winds. You pick up your pace. You are horrified to discover three men pinned down by the weight of a bundle of cables. The clamp holding it in place must have broken when the bundle jerked. It has pinned John Anderson down by the legs, John Erickson by the hips, and John Eastman by the chest.

"Call a rescue team," you shout to your workmate while you go see if there is anything you can do to help.

The cables are too heavy for you to move, so the best you can do is comfort the men. You give them some water and tell them how angry Strauss will be if they die.

"He's been a stickler for safety," you say, rapping your hard hat. "No one has died on the bridge yet, and I hear he's even stringing a safety net under the roadway for when construction starts on it."

These workers are bundling wires to a main cable. Each main bridge cable is made up of 27,572 individual wires.

Turn the page.

Because of the weather, the rescue team doesn't arrive for half an hour. Then it's almost another hour before the cable is lifted off the men.

You help carry Erickson on a stretcher down to a waiting ambulance. All three men will eventually recover from their wounds.

"Quick thinking," your crew boss says as he pats you on the back.

In May 1936 the cables between the bridges are finished. Your work is completed. Because of the excellent work you've done, you are offered a job working on the bridge's roadway. You've stayed safe on the bridge so far, but you wonder if it would be better for your next job to be on a less dangerous construction project.

To accept the job on the roadway, go to page 85.

To quit work on the bridge because it's too dangerous, turn to page 91.

With the Great Depression still causing much suffering around the world, you don't want to say no to a job no matter how dangerous it is.

Actually, you've been surprised at how few serious injuries have occurred on the Golden Gate Bridge. Usually, it is estimated that for every $1 million a project costs, there will be one death. But at a cost of $35 million, there has only been one fatality on this project. On October 21, 1936, Kermit Moore died when a crane accidently fell on him.

It has helped that Joseph Strauss has required hard hats for ironworkers and masks with respirators for anyone exposed to toxic fumes. And Strauss even had a safety net set up under the bridge for anyone working on the roadway.

Turn the page.

As you work on riveting together the beams that will support the roadway, you look down at the safety net. So far, a handful of men have fallen into it. They jokingly consider themselves members of an exclusive club, because they cheated death.

The enormous roadway safety net cost $130,000. It eventually saved 19 men from falling.

Beyond the safety net is the ice-cold water of the Golden Gate strait. You think about how much it hurts to belly flop into a pool. To fall from this height, more than 200 feet, the water would feel like landing on concrete. Serious injury or death would be the likely result of such a fall.

On the morning of February 17, 1937, your workday starts like any normal day. You wind your way up through the metal girders, always being careful of your step. Things are especially dangerous in the mornings when mist from the fog slickens the beams. Add to that the typical gusts of wind, and a groggy worker could easily find himself falling down into the net.

Turn the page.

Construction on the roadway is nearly complete and your foreman, Slim, has your crew taking down the planking that is under the bridge. Things need to be cleaned up to prepare for the opening of the bridge next month.

Everything is going well, until the section you are standing on starts shaking. You are about to shout to Slim when there is a deafening metallic screech. Then the world drops out from underneath you.

To let yourself fall into the safety net, turn to page 96.

To try to jump to a nearby beam, turn to page 98.

You put on a T-shirt, along with protective clothing like overalls, boots, and gloves. The weather is a little foggy in the morning, but you're sure things will warm up as the sun burns off the fog.

Since you have a new job, you decide to celebrate by paying to ride the trolley to Fort Point. Once there, you quickly find your crew boss.

He just shakes his head when he sees what you're wearing. He has on a thick, heavy coat and a sweater under that. And you even notice pieces of crumbled-up newspaper peeking out from under his clothes.

"You've never worked on a bridge this big before, have you?" he asks.

"No, sir," you reply.

"It shows," he says.

Turn the page.

You are then taken over to the south tower with the rest of your crew. You ride up an elevator to your work site. Once up hundreds of feet, you understand why your crew boss was dressed in such heavy clothes. The weather isn't as warm as you expected. It's actually quite cold. Gusts of wind whip around like cold ropes, stinging any exposed skin.

You don't make it more than a few hours before you are sent back down. Your teeth are chattering. Your arms are purple and covered in goose bumps. And you can tell by the disgusted look on your crew boss' face that he doesn't want you back.

Without a job, you worry that you and your family are going to go hungry.

THE END

To follow another path, turn to page 11.
To read the conclusion, turn to page 101.

The country is still in the midst of the Great Depression. But your work on the Golden Gate Bridge provided you with valuable experience.

Construction on the Bay Bridge connecting San Francisco to Oakland began in 1933. Ironworkers are needed there too. While you'll have to get up earlier and travel farther to work in the morning, you hear weather conditions aren't quite as dangerous on that bridge. So you get a job working on it.

By the time the job is completed in 1936 you have saved enough money to buy a brand new car—a Ford Cabriolet. In 1937 you pay 50 cents to drive your family across the Golden Gate Bridge. As you do you proudly point out the sections high in the towers that you helped build.

THE END

To follow another path, turn to page 11.
To read the conclusion, turn to page 101.

You don't want to get caught off guard if the wheels come racing toward you. If the wires get tangled, or if they aren't properly placed, hours of work could be lost.

Some workers wore glare-free goggles to help them see through the sun reflecting off the water below.

So you wait.

And wait.

Surrounded by fog with a deafening wind whistling in your ears, it's hard to judge time. You feel like you've waited for hours. No wheels.

Then, from the top of the tower, you hear muffled screams through the roar of the wind. You rush up the catwalk to the top of the tower. There, to your horror, you see some of your crew trying to help three men who are pinned under the bundle of cables. The clamp that had held it in place must have broken. John Anderson is pinned down by the legs, John Erickson by the hips, and the cable is laying across John Eastman's chest. You rush to the aid of the injured men.

Turn the page.

Anderson and Erickson are closest to you, so you make a split-second decision to help them first. But as you focus in on Eastman, you're afraid that you should have helped him first. The weight of the bundle of cables is slowly making it more and more difficult for him to breathe. And no matter how hard you and the workers around you try, you cannot move the heavy cables from his chest.

Because of the high winds, it takes a rescue team nearly half an hour to get to the top of the tower. Then it takes them an hour to get the cables lifted off the men.

You help carry Anderson down from the tower on a stretcher and load him into an ambulance. He and Erickson eventually recover from their injuries.

Eastman survives too, but because of how long he was under the cable, he doesn't fully recover.

You go back to your job and help in creating the world's largest bridge, but you think back to that day for the rest of your life. If only you'd been a little quicker to help Eastman, you might have been able to prevent him from experiencing such severe injuries.

THE END

To follow another path, turn to page 11.
To read the conclusion, turn to page 101.

You fall along with most of your crew.

For a brief moment, you think you're safe as you hit the net. But the weight of the planks and beams that broke loose rips right through it. You keep falling, screaming.

The scaffold structure that ripped the net on February 17, 1937, weighed about 5 tons.

Your body is slammed against the surface of the water. Pain explodes all over you as ribs are crushed and muscles are wrenched. Your body feels broken from hitting the water after the fall. You struggle to clear your head, but you feel hazy with shock. Looking up, you see debris falling toward you. Feeling numb from the cold, you realize you can't swim anymore. Moments later you lose consciousness and slip below the white-capped waters of the Bay.

On that fatal day, you are one of 10 people who die, raising the Golden Gate Bridge's death count to 11.

THE END

To follow another path, turn to page 11.
To read the conclusion, turn to page 101.

You reach out and grab a nearby beam. Below, the beams that broke away from the bridge tear through the net. Workers scream as they fall hundreds of feet and crash into the water. Deadly debris rains down on them.

You hang there for a few moments. Then you pull yourself up onto the beam. Looking around, you see two of your crewmates, Pete and Larry. They are staring down at the water, dumbfounded.

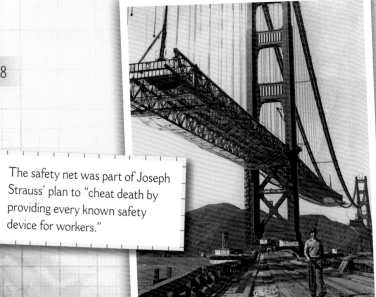

The safety net was part of Joseph Strauss' plan to "cheat death by providing every known safety device for workers."

Slim was one of the lucky ones who survived the fall. He was picked up by boat. Of the 12 workers who fell into the strait, only one other survived. Though this accident increased the bridge's death toll to 11, its safety record is still better than other major construction projects done recently. Twenty-four workers died on the Bay Bridge, which was completed just a year earlier. At least 27 died while the Brooklyn Bridge was under construction.

The Golden Gate Bridge opens a few months later. Over the years of working on the bridge, you have been able to save enough money to buy a car. On the day the bridge opens to traffic, you happily pay the 50-cent toll to drive your family across.

THE END

To follow another path, turn to page 11.
To read the conclusion, turn to page 101.

Pedestrians were thrilled to cross the bridge for the first time.

CHAPTER 4

STANDING THE TEST OF TIME

On May 27, 1937, people lined up on a cold, foggy morning to be among the first to cross the Golden Gate Bridge. Nearly 200,000 people walked, danced, and ran from the San Francisco end to the Marin County side during the opening day celebrations. The next day, the bridge opened to vehicle traffic. During its first full year more than 33 million cars crossed the bridge. Drivers paid a 50-cent toll each way. Today an estimated 40 million cars use the bridge each year. An average of 100,000 cars drive over the bridge every day. The toll of $6 is collected only for vehicles traveling south into San Francisco.

The Golden Gate Bridge was one of the largest construction projects of its kind when completed. It is listed among the top 10 construction achievements of the 20th century. Also on the list is New York City's Empire State Building which was the world's tallest building from 1931 to 1970.

In 1951 high winds caused damage to some of the bridge's cables.

Any structure the size of the Golden Gate Bridge needs repairs to keep it in good condition. It has gone through several upgrades over the years. In 1951, wind gusts reached 69 miles per hour and caused the bridge to sway perilously. It was closed to traffic for several hours. Over the next few years, additional bracing beams were added to stiffen the bridge's roadway. Then in 1989 an earthquake measuring a magnitude of 7.1 on the Richter scale rattled the Bay area. The bridge was not damaged, but inspectors said the towers needed strengthening. The bridge has since been retrofitted with new parts that not only make it stronger but also allow it to adjust to the movements an earthquake creates. Now it is estimated that the bridge could withstand an 8.3-magnitude earthquake.

The bridge suffers from the wear and tear of more than 40 million cars crossing it yearly. In the 1980s the entire roadway was replaced. But the Bay's environment is even more damaging than the traffic. Seawater causes metal to rust, and the harsh weather of the Bay area is very damaging to the bridge. As rivets weaken, a team of ironworkers replaces them with stronger bolts.

Workers still climb to the top of the bridge to keep its paint in good condition.

The most costly repairs involve repainting the bridge. Harsh weather constantly wears away at the paint. Paint protects the bridge from rusting. Touch-up work needs to be done on an ongoing basis and costs millions of dollars.

The Golden Gate Bridge remains a symbolic and internationally recognized monument. It had the longest main span of any suspension bridge in the world from its opening in 1937 until 1964. It has even been declared a Wonder of the Modern World by the American Society of Civil Engineers.

When investors asked Joseph Strauss how long the bridge would last, he responded, "Forever!" He believed that if cared for properly, it would have "life without end." Nearly 80 years after its construction, the Golden Gate Bridge is still functioning as Joseph Strauss imagined it.

TIMELINE

1872—Railroad executive Charles Crocker proposes the idea of building a bridge over the Golden Gate.

1904—Joseph Strauss founds the Strauss Bascule Bridge Company.

1915—Michael O'Shaughnessy hires Joseph Strauss for a project in San Francisco.

1916—James Wilkins writes an article in the *San Francisco Call Bulletin* imagining a bridge to connect Marin and San Francisco counties.

1919—Joseph Strauss visits with Michael O'Shaughnessy to discuss the feasibility of building a bridge over the Golden Gate.

1921—Joseph Strauss presents his initial design of a cantilever-suspension hybrid bridge to O'Shaughnessy. This design will change over time.

1923—The Golden Gate Bridge and Highway District is established to oversee the planning and financing of a bridge spanning the Golden Gate.

1924—The War Department approves Joseph Strauss' original bridge design.

1929—The Board of Supervisors appoints Joseph Strauss to be chief engineer of the Golden Gate Bridge and sets up an Advisory Board of Engineers. This is also the year that the stock market crashes, setting off the Great Depression.

1930—Joseph Strauss turns in his final plans for a suspension bridge to the Golden Gate Bridge and Highway District.

1931—Joseph Strauss fires Charles Ellis. Some sources say it was because Strauss wasn't happy with how quickly Ellis was finishing his calculations. Clifford Paine is hired to replace Ellis.

1933—Construction begins.

1934—North (Marin) tower is completed.

1935—South (San Francisco) tower is completed.

1936—Construction of the middle span of the bridge and the roadway begins.

1937—The Golden Gate Bridge opens to the public with a 50-cent toll.

1951—High winds cause the bridge to close. Bracing beams are added to stiffen the bridge's roadway.

1968—The Golden Gate Bridge's toll is changed so that only southbound traffic (traffic flowing into San Francisco) has to pay.

1989—A 7.1-magnitude earthquake rattles the Bay area and creates concerns about what a stronger earthquake might do to the bridge. Over the years that follow, the bridge is retrofitted to better handle earthquakes.

2008—The bridge toll is raised to $6.

OTHER PATHS TO EXPLORE

In this book you've seen how the events of the past look different from two points of view. Perspectives on history are as varied as the people who lived it. Seeing history from many points of view is an important part of understanding it. Here are some ideas for other Golden Gate Bridge points of view to explore:

+ People living in the Bay area in the 1930s had conflicting views about the bridge. Discuss some of the reasons why people were in favor of it, and some of the reasons they might have opposed the project.
  (Key Ideas and Details)

+ The Golden Gate Bridge took four years and $35 million to construct. Compare the cost and time and labor it took to construct the bridge in the 1930s to some more recent bridge projects throughout the world. How do they compare?
  (Integration of Knowledge and Ideas)

READ MORE

Hurley, Michael. *The World's Most Amazing Bridges.* Landmark Top Tens. Chicago: Raintree, 2012.

Latham, Donna. *Bridges and Tunnels: Investigate Feats of Engineering.* White River Junction, Vt.: Nomad Press, 2012.

Wearing, Judy, and Tom Riddolls. *Golden Gate Bridge.* New York: AV2, 2014.

INTERNET SITES

FactHound offers a safe, fun way to find Internet sites related to this book. All of the sites on FactHound have been researched by our staff.

Here's all you do:

Visit *www.facthound.com*

Type in this code: 9781491403983

GLOSSARY

cantilever bridge (can-tih-LEV-ur BRIJ)—a bridge that is supported by arms balancing on support towers

hybrid (HYE-brid)—a mix of two different types

magnitude (MAG-nuh-tood)—a measure of the amount of energy released by an earthquake

retrofit (RET-troh-fit)—to modify an original structure by adding something to it that improves the structure in some way

Richter scale (RIK-tur SKALE)—a scale that measures the amount of energy in an earthquake

rivet (RIV-it)—a strong metal bolt that is used to fasten something together

rust (RUHST)—a red-brown substance that forms on iron and steel when they are exposed to water or air

suspension bridge (suh-SPEN-shuhn BRIJ)—a bridge that is hung from cables strung between support towers

toll (TOHL)—a charge for using a bridge or roadway

BIBLIOGRAPHY

Adams, Charles F. *Heroes of the Golden Gate.* Palo Alto, Calif.: Pacific Books, 1987.

Brown, Allen. *Golden Gate, Biography of a Bridge.* Garden City, N.Y.: Doubleday, 1965.

Cassady, Stephen. *Baron Wolman Presents Spanning the Gate.* Mill Valley, Calif.: Squarebooks, 1979.

Golden Gate Bridge Research Library. 23 April, 2014. http://goldengatebridge.org/research

Liberatore, Karen. *The Complete Guide to the Golden Gate National Recreation Area.* San Francisco: Chronicle Books, 1982.

National Park Services: Golden Gate National Recreation Area. 23 April, 2014. http://www.nps.gov/goga/index.htm

PBS: Golden Gate Bridge. 23 April, 2014. http://www.pbs.org/wgbh/americanexperience/films/goldengate

Starr, Kevin. *Golden Gate: The Life and Times of America's Greatest Bridge.* New York: Bloomsbury Press, 2010.

Van der Zee, John. *The Gate: The True Story of the Design and Construction of the Golden Gate Bridge.* New York: Simon and Schuster, 1986.

INDEX